GETTING EVEN MORE HELP FROM YOUR DOGS

More Ways to Gain Insights, Advice, Power and Other Help Using the Dog Type System

by Gini Graham Scott, Ph.D.
Author of *Do You Look Like Your Dog?*

GETTING EVEN MORE HELP FROM YOUR DOGS

Copyright © 2017 by Gini Graham Scott

All rights reserved. No part of this book may be used or reproduced by any means, graphic, electronic, or mechanical, including photocopying, recording, taping or by any information storage retrieval system without the written permission of the author except in the case of brief quotations embodied in critical articles and reviews.

TABLE OF CONTENTS

INTRODUCTION 5
CHAPTER 1: MAKING CHANGES: "TEACHING AN OLD DOG NEW TRICKS" 7
   The Need to Be Flexible 7
   An Example of One Man's Self-Transformation 9
   How You Can Change Your Basic Personality Traits 10
   Creating a Better Balance in Your Personality Traits or Expressing Them 12
   Here's How It Works 14
   The Four Steps to Change 17
   Determining How You Want to Change 19
   Recognizing What or Who You Want to Become 22
   Changing Your Overall Personality Orientation and Specific Traits . 26
   Using Mental Scripting to See Yourself As You Want to Be 26
CHAPTER 2: TECHNIQUES TO UNDERSTAND AND IMPROVE YOUR RELATIONSHIPS 31
   Getting a Quick First Impression About the People You Meet 31
   Getting First Impressions 34
   Getting Advance Impressions of Someone Before You Meet 35
   Gaining In-Depth Insight into Others 36
   Using Visualization and Dog Profiling Techniques to Improve Your Relationships 49
   Increasing Your Power in a Relationship 54
   Influencing Your Relationships in Other Ways 56
CHAPTER 3: A WORKSHOP ON WORKING WITH YOUR GUIDE DOG 59
   The Workshop Setting 59
   Meeting One's Guide Dog (or Dogs) 60
   Getting Help from One's Guide Dogs 62
   Gaining Insights about Another Person 64
   Getting First Impressions 67
   An Exercise on Getting First Impressions 69
   A Day of Seeing Dogs 71
   Learning from the Dog Associations 74
   Making Changes in a Relationship 76
   Setting Up Your Own Workshop 80

INTRODUCTION

The first two books in the Dog Type series were devoted to learning about the profiles of different types of dogs and about the five most common types of dog helpers.

As previously described in *Discovering Your Dog Type,* there are about three dozen categories of dogs, classified as working, herding, sporting, non-sporting, terriers, hounds, and toy dogs. You can use the dogs you like best and least or associate with others to better understand yourself and others. This knowledge will contribute to better communication and relationships.

As described in *Getting Help from Your Dogs,* the five types of helper dogs include your Top Dog, Watch Dog, Underdog, Guide Dog, and Power Dog. You can call on their help in various ways. For example, look to your Top Dog for general support, your Watch Dog to help you stay safe, and your Underdog to show you where you are weak or lack skills so you can build yourself up. Your Guide Dogs are useful for advice, and your Power Dogs help you feel more powerful and exercise your power wisely. A series of exercises help you contact and get to know these helper dogs and call on them to help you better deal with everyday problems and issues.

Getting Even More Help from Your Dogs provides you with additional ways to work with your dogs, along with a Rescue Dog, who can step in when you need more help.

The following chapters discuss a variety of techniques for more success in whatever you do, including having better relationships with others. The first chapter deals with ways to make changes in yourself and in your life by calling on different helper dogs. The process is like having several assistants on staff to call on for help with different types of problems.

The next chapter focuses on better understanding others by using the dog types, such as when you get a first impression or want more insights into that person. The chapter also discusses how to increase your power in relating to others.

The last chapter describes a workshop I did to help others apply these methods to improving their lives.

CHAPTER 1: MAKING CHANGES: "TEACHING AN OLD DOG NEW TRICKS"

Once you know who you want to be, the next step is deciding what to do to get there, with the help of whichever members of your team – your Top Dog, Watch Dog, Underdog, Guide Dogs, or Power Dogs – you want to use under the circumstances. Consider these options like having a team of corporate advisors and employees from all levels of the organization. You select the team you want for a particular project.

This chapter draws on techniques for changing yourself, which I discussed in several books dealing with creativity and visualization. These include: *Mind Power: Picture Your Way to Success; The Empowered Mind: How to Harness the Creative Force Within You,* and *Want It, See It, Get It!* Here the techniques are applied to help you in gaining additional help with the assistance of your Dog Team.

The Need to Be Flexible

Being able to make changes in your personality or style is especially important in today's rapidly changing global world, so you can play different roles in different situations with different people. For example, you may be Bulldog tough with some people, soft and gentle like a Poodle with others. You may be all business like a stern German Shepherd with associates and in some situations; wild and crazy like an eager Pomeranian with friends when it comes time to party. Whatever your primary traits, reflected in your Top Dog or Watch Dog choices, you can adopt other traits as needed by imagining you are with or supported by the type of dog you would like to be. For example, visualize yourself having the power of the Bullmastiff as you go into a tense meeting, or the style and confidence of an Afghan Hound at an art gallery opening.

As you think about your own situation, you'll find many times when it helps to change your personal style to meet new role requirements with different people and in unfamiliar situations. So you can call on the dogs to help. Just decide what kind of person you want to be in the situation; then ask the appropriate dog to assist. You can use the Chart "Determining What Personality Trait to Change and How".

Some typical situations might be:
- You are asked to take charge and aren't sure what to do.
- You have to make a career change, and the culture of the new field is different from the one you are leaving.
- You are working with a new group of people with different values and expectations and want to get along.
- You want to advance to a new position with different tasks and roles.

All such changes mean learning to act in a new way, perhaps change your image, and bring out a hidden side of you. That's where understanding yourself based on your Top Dog, Watch Dog, and Underdog preferences can help you clarify your strongest qualities and how you want to change.

This first category of change reflects "positive" or "pull" changes — things you want to move toward. Alternatively, the things you want to stop doing represent "negative" or "push" changes – things you want to reject. For example:
- You are too shy and unassertive to get what you want or get ahead.
- You are often difficult to work with, since you are too sensitive and irritable.
- You are too pushy and aggressive, so people you would like to work with are often afraid of you or try to avoid you.

In short, for whatever reason, you can make changes to better fit in, get along, or otherwise get what you want. And you can and will. As the popular expression goes, you are "teaching the old dog new tricks."

An Example of One Man's Self-Transformation

Here's an example of how you might use the process, based on how one man made changes. He used his Dog Team to help facilitate the process.

In this case, Sam was a fairly shy and bookish guy, when he worked as a systems engineer in the high-tech field. People looked up to him for his knowledge, and his boss praised him for his quiet persistence and conscientiousness. Outwardly, there was a good fit between Sam's work and how he behaved. Perhaps he was like a quiet, well-behaved Pekingese.

However, Sam was unsure of himself with people, and often he didn't feel at ease going to parties and making small talk. On his job this lack of social skills didn't matter, because his employers were more interested in his technical designs than how he interacted with others.

For several years, nothing changed. Sam imagined it would be nice to be more outgoing and comfortable in social settings, but he did nothing about it, since he had created a comfortable niche for himself –like a dog having a cozy warm box in the basement.

Then, due to company cutbacks, Sam suddenly found himself out of work in a super-tight jobs market. So he *had* to change, not because he wanted to be different, but for economic survival.

After reviewing his strengths and weaknesses, he felt a good combo might be combining his technical skills with the social skills he wanted to develop, so he could market high tech products. But he was starting off with no sales and people skills. So he had to make himself over to step into this new role.

At first, Sam was very nervous about approaching people to sell them anything. But he began imagining himself in this role and practicing at home in front of his mirror – a good time to call on his Dog Team for extra help. He envisioned himself taking on the qualities of a warm, friendly, social, yet powerful dog – a Great Dane – to see himself in this leadership role. He imagined the dog beside him, supporting him as he practiced, and visualized himself becoming that dog to feel those qualities.

Such practice was just what Sam needed, and finally he mustered up enough courage to start interviewing. As a result, he landed a job in telemarketing. Later, as he gained more confidence through his work on the phone and continued visualization and mirror practice at home, he got a job as an outside rep. Gradually, he moved from *playing* the role of the enthusiastic high-tech marketing rep to being in the role. At the same time, his more outgoing personality at work carried over into his personal life, and he was more comfortable in social situations. He gradually left his shyness behind as he became accustomed to working with people every day. Thus, after a while, he was no longer the shy bookish systems engineer but had become the knowledgeable, friendly high-tech marketing rep, and that felt good.

How You Can Change Your Basic Personality Traits

Sam's dramatic change — from normally shy introvert to outgoing extrovert— illustrates that you can change your most basic personality traits when necessary. Although we develop certain traits due to our experience dating back to childhood — and certain traits may feel more comfortable, so we think that's "our nature", in fact, we are very plastic. As a result, we can adapt in many ways. Even a 180-degree transformation may come to seem very natural after a while – such as switching from being like an affable, relaxed Pug to being more like a proud, self-assured Irish Wolfhound. Alternatively, say you're an overly aggressive, impulsive Bull Terrier type, which has worked well for you as a self-staring entrepreneur. But now you're taking on a corporate job. Perhaps becoming more like a placid, determined Blood Hound might better suit the work culture in a conservative corporate setting.

Whatever the changes you might cultivate, a good reason for developing this other side of yourself is that you can then shift back and forth, choosing whichever style is more appropriate in a particular situation. Or in other cases, the new style is best suited for replacing the way you were, and you have made a permanent alteration in your life.

The key to making this personal transformation successfully is to determine the personality traits that no longer work in your new setting and figure out the qualities you need to adopt to be successful in these changed circumstances. That's where your Dog Team can help – helping you zero in on the qualities you want and don't want and supporting your efforts to change. Then, with a little help from your Dog Friends, you can work on practicing such traits. For example, if, like Sam, you have to learn to be more outgoing and comfortable with people, you would do things like:

- Put yourself in social situations, like cocktail parties and professional mixers, and force yourself to meet and talk to people. (Imagining an especially friendly member of your Dog Team beside you can help you push yourself to be more outgoing in this anxiety-producing situation).
- Volunteer to do things in a social organization that forces you to relate to people, such as helping to set up programs and introduce speakers, hosting at meetings, and doing publicity for the group. (Seeing yourself as a dog with a reputation for assisting, like a St. Bernard, can help).

Alternatively, to become more introspective and thoughtful, you would put yourself in situations such as:

- Go for a weekend retreat at a calm, peaceful location.(And to calm down even more, imagine yourself as normally laid back, calm dog like a Labrador);
- Volunteer to do Internet research for an organization. (And for support in your research role, imagine you are closing in on your quarry like one of the scent hounds; like a Blood Hound).

You can use the chart on the following page to help you identify traits that no longer work in your new situation, determine the traits you need to adopt, and consider what to do to become more comfortable with this new style of relating.

DETERMINING WHAT PERSONALITY TRAITS TO CHANGE AND HOW					
New Situation Requiring Change	Differences in New Situation	Personality Traits That Aren't Working – and the Dog Breed Associated with Those Traits	Personality Traits I Need to Develop – and the Dog Breed Associated with Those Traits	What Can I Do to Develop These Traits – And How My Dog Team Can Help Me

Creating a Better Balance in Your Personality Traits or Expressing Them

Another way to change yourself is to create a better balance in the traits you have or become more aware of when you express different traits, to use them more appropriately. You need to be able to use one trait in certain contexts and a different trait in others, so you can better respond to the wide range of circumstances in your daily life. The process is like learning to not only become an actor, but to be a great one. In the process, you become better at calling on and controlling your Dog Team, like guiding a team of sled dogs through the frozen arctic. You choose the best dogs to be on your sled to help you win the race.

This is what Paul had to do. He was the coordinator of a large volunteer organization, and the members loved him because he was so compassionate and caring. They also liked his casual spontaneity that put people immediately at ease. He was like a warm, loving Collie or Shetland Sheepdog.

Yet, too much of a good thing created problems in managing the group, because he was often too nice, spontaneous, and disorganized. Since he wanted so much to help people and be liked, he sometimes lacked the necessary discipline to control some members. At one point he even tried an ill-fated experiment in democracy that led some people in the group to rebel against his authority and try to run the program themselves. Also, at times, he was so playful at meetings – like a cuddly, eager puppy — that instead of creating a warm rapport between people he became annoying and disruptive. In addition, his disorganization sometimes led him to lose important documents or fail to follow-up on important leads.

Paul's need was not to stop being nice, caring, and spontaneous, but to better control these traits and balance them with a greater assertiveness, firmness, and order. In effect, he needed to combine his warm, friendly Collie or Shetland Sheepdog with some infusion of Mastiff and Great Dane.

Thus, realizing what he needed to do, Paul began to alter his personality. He still kept the warm, friendly, playful traits that endeared him to people and motivated members to remain involved. But he toned them down, so they were more controlled, and he became more direct and forceful with staffers when necessary. As a result, he reestablished his authority and undercut a growing "let's take over the organization" movement that would have undermined the group. Additionally, realizing he needed help in getting more organized, he got some people who were detail oriented to help organize his office, and he set up a system to track his papers and the tasks he needed to do. He learned to control his tendency to be funny and playful at inappropriate times. And he made changes in his thinking and attitude by visualizing himself acting differently.

Once you make the changes you need to reinforce and correct those changes, they stick. To reinforce his changed way of thinking, Paul could use an image of the dog linked to the desired trait as a trigger to act that way. For instance, to release his warm, friendly side, Paul could think to himself, "Now I'm a Collie" or "I'm putting on my Shetland Sheepdog." Or to step into the tough, more forceful role, he could say to himself: "Now I'm a Mastiff" or "I'm putting on my Great Dane." Or perhaps Paul could use a physical visual image as a reminder, such as putting on a hat with the picture of a Collie to bring out his softer, playful side, versus using a picture of a Great Dane to show his tougher, no-nonsense side. Or instead of a picture, he could use a ceramic sculpture, postcard, poster, or other form of reminder. Then, over time, like a conditioned response, just seeing the image could become an automatic trigger for him to act in a certain way. In short, you internalize the role and soon act that way without thinking about it – thanks to your Reminder Dog.

Here's How It Works

Here are two examples to illustrate how to "call on your dogs" when you need help in changing yourself. One is based on a personal experience; the other from a job situation.

Example #1: A Conflict with a Family Member

Say you are having a conflict with a family member – let's call him Jack. Whenever you see each other, you both tend to rub each other the wrong way. You say something, Jack responds, you make some insulting comment, and soon the argument is on, disrupting the family gathering and almost leading to blows before people pull you apart. Yet, you can't avoid seeing each other, because there will always be that family gathering. Here's how calling on the dogs might help.

First, suppose looking at your profile, you see that your Top Dog is a Jack Russell Terrier and your Watch Dog is a Norwich Terrier; both fairly feisty dogs. By contrast, your underdog is a Bassett Hound, which you consider a sad-eyed, slow-moving dog. Well, maybe you need to work on taming your Top Dog and Watch

Dog so you can and bring out more of your usually repressed Bassett Hound qualities. Then, you might be less likely to react so quickly.

Yet, suppose you still aren't sure what to do, so you call on one of your helpful Guide Dogs, a wise old Yellow Labrador. He sits quietly and listens, as you use self-talk –having a conversation with yourself, though you imagine you're talking to your Yellow Lab.

Then, you listen to some of his suggestions. "Whatever you do, don't engage…You don't have to respond… Don't try to one-up Jack. You'll only increase his anger…You don't have to get angry no matter what he says…When you feel insulted by Jack, don't think you have to respond to save face…Just smile to acknowledge the comment…Say something like: 'Sure, you're welcome to your opinion…Then walk away…" and so on.

In such a conversation with your Guide Dog, you may get a string of different suggestions of what to do, how to feel, and how to respond. As you hear them, write them down, to remember them, and later you can choose among them. You can use the previous Chart "Determining What Personality Traits to Change and How" to help you go through this process.

Then, when you check about what to do when you meet Jack again, your Power Dog might help by being with you in the situation. Or possibly you may experience yourself becoming or putting on that Power Dog to help you deal with that situation, such as helping you work out a plan for how to respond or not respond. You might even try some role plays to practice what you will do in the future.

So now you are in the situation, where Jack is making his usual insulting remarks and putting you down in his usual sly way and boy are you mad. You know you shouldn't respond; you've told yourself to walk away, and that you need to be more like a laid-back Bassett Hound, rather than your usual Jack Russell Terrier self. But for you that's hard. You know you should go, but you really want to stay and fight.

Then it's your Power Dog, a big husky St. Bernard, to the rescue. Just as you are ready to stab with a sharp zinger comment, you gradually withdraw, and finally pull back. Whew! Another family fight averted. A little later, as you grab a drink at the buffet table, you imagine your St. Bernard giving you that well-deserved drink as a reward for staying out of the fray. Later still, whenever you see Jack at a family get-together and feel ready to go over to resume the combat, you think of your St. Bernard just behind you, pulling you back, so you resist the urge, and this time there's no heated family fight.

Example #2: A Problem with a Co-Worker

Say your problem at work is a co-worker, Judy, who gets all the glory. She is more outgoing and knows what to say to get on the best side of your boss. Yet, you have been doing much of the work and giving Judy advice on how to do her job, so she looks even better. But you don't know how to get more recognition that might lead to more money and a promotion for yourself without coming across as a complainer, and worse, jeopardize your position, because your boss thinks so highly of your co-worker.

What to do? You start by looking at your profile, which shows your Top Dog is a soft, cuddly Pug; your Watch Dog is a lively, affectionate Pomeranian, who loves to be loved, and your Underdog is a Pit Bull, because you think of it as a vicious attack dog. That profile is a good clue for what's not working for you at work – you are too eager to be helpful and loved and don't stick up enough for yourself. You are letting yourself be a pushover because of your need to belong, be accepted, and be thought good. You have essentially chosen to be a "lap dog" which is fine when you make a great companion for someone who reciprocates your friendship and affection. But you can easily be taken advantage of, as in this situation, and that's when you need to be more of a Pit Bull and unleash the qualities you may not like, but need to apply now.

Once you have made this assessment, the next step is to figure out what to do, and that's when you can get help from your Guide Dogs. In this case, you take some time at home to reflect on what's happening at the office and what to do and ask your two Guide Dogs for advice. One is a Siberian Husky, known for being independent, willful, very intelligent, and a good team player; the other is a strong, solid Chow Chow. As you reflect on what to do, you get different insights by asking questions and hearing different suggestions; like listening to a conversation in your head. For example, some of the suggestions are: "Be firm...You need to get credit for what you have done...Don't let Judy take advantage of you...Find a way to get credit without complaining...Continue to help but ask for credit when you do."

Eventually, as a result of this reflection, you come up with a plan for the next time Judy asks for some assistance. You will be glad to help, even take extra time to do a really good job. But in return, you want to be included at the meetings with the boss to discuss the project. This way, you can tell Judy you will know firsthand what needs to be done (and though you don't say this, by being at the meeting, your boss will know that you are contributing, and if you ask good questions and make good suggestions about what to do, your boss will recognize your valuable contribution.) And if Judy doesn't want you there, be prepared to say no to helping her. In other words, if she wants your help, you need to get the credit for what you are doing. If not, no help.

Then, once you have decided what to do, you might practice how you will act in a future encounter with Judy.

After that, your Power Dog can help. Though you've got your plan in mind, when you talk to Judy, you want some extra support, so call on your Power Dog to come with you. In this case, it's a big strong Alaskan Malamute, a dog that wants to be helpful and is a great team player, but it won't take any flak from anyone. In other words, if Judy wants your help in pulling the sled, she has to make you a co-captain. You're not going to help and stand behind the sled anymore, watching it race away after you've help to load it.

The Four Steps to Change

Now that you've got the general idea of how this change process works, here's how to change yourself to take on the personality or play the role you want. The four steps to change are:

1. Determine how you want to change; what or who you want to become.
To do this, think about the traits of your Top Dog, Watch Dog, and Underdog. That process will help to highlight those qualities you want and those you don't; then the qualities of your Underdog may be just what you need to develop to help you act differently to achieve your goals.

2. Decide how to act in a particular situation in the future to express these changes.
Now, use self-talk to have a conversation with yourself about your options, and what you might best do in a particular situation. As you do, call on your Guide Dogs for their input and advice. Also, you can imagine yourself enacting your plan and create a mental script to see yourself in this new role. Then, see yourself doing whatever you ideally would like to do in the future. Also, you can envision other likely outcomes and see yourself respond in varying circumstances. In short, plan what to do in varying scenarios, so you are better able to respond and guide the process in reality.

3. Practice what to do in the future.
Now, besides imagining what might be likely to happen and what to do in your imagination, practice in reality. Practice exercising self-control and politely walking away when a jerky relative starts to engage you in an argument; rehearse how to confront that co-worker who is using your work without giving you credit.
Through the rehearsal process, you not only act out a new way of responding, but you reinforce this new desired image you want of yourself – and this new image of you will carry over into other situations.
In some case, you may not have time to use this step, since you have to quickly turn your plan into action. But ideally, take time to try out this new way of being and acting, since this will give you greater confidence when you actually play out the role – much like

an actor feels more self-assured after practicing rather than trusting to a quick read and spontaneous action to produce a good performance.

4. <u>Play out your plan or mental script in actual practice</u>.

Now it's time for action. You have thought through what you need to change, have developed your plan or mental script, and if possible, have rehearsed. Now, lights, camera, action – you're ready to perform. And this is where your Power Dog can help by cheering you on, so you confidently act in this new way.

Initially, when you act in this different way, it may feel like an act, and that's fine. Then, as you continue to act– possibly with the continued help of your Power Dog reminding you to play this new role and supporting this effort, you will increasingly find this new way of action familiar and comfortable. In time, you will internalize this new way of being as part of you, so you not only act the part, but feel the part. When this happens, you may find you have a new Top Dog, Watch Dog, and Underdog, too, because you have really changed, and as a result, your chosen dogs may change as well.

Determining How You Want to Change

Besides changing in response to particular situations, you can make more general changes, again with some help from your Dog Team. Start by asking yourself: "How would I like to change? What or who do I want to become?"

Think about what aspects of your personality you don't like and imagine their opposite. Say, if you feel you are too quiet and retiring, like a Bassett Hound; think about what it would be like to be more assertive and outgoing, like a Bullmastiff. If you feel you are too standoffish and reserved, imagine yourself participating more, like a warm and friendly Golden Retriever or being cheery and comical like a Chinese Shorthaired Crested. If you lack confidence, see yourself as an assured, confident Dalmatian, regally seated on a fire truck as it passes through town.

In short, change the picture of yourself with the qualities you don't want to a picture of yourself possessing the qualities you hope to have. Use the dog you associate with that image, such as one of your Power Dogs, as a reminder of the qualities you want to acquire.

Exercise: Changing the Qualities You Don't Want to Those You Do

One approach to making changes is with the Transforming Unwanted into Wanted Qualities Chart, if you like doing things in a more logical, organized way. In column one, list those qualities you would like to change, then the qualities you don't want to have. List them as they occur to you; don't try to edit or analyze them. Then, go down column two and for each one, list an opposite or different quality – the ones you would like to have to replace the qualities listed in column one. Write down the first quality that comes to mind so you keep your responses spontaneous.

Finally, for each pair, create a picture in which you see yourself in a scene with the original quality. Again, let the picture come to you spontaneously. Then, imagine that this picture is suddenly being torn up, and see yourself with the opposite or a different quality. Experience yourself possessing this quality for about a minute. Repeat the visualizations of yourself with these new qualities over the next few days, and try putting each one into practice. As you go through this exercise, your dogs can help in various ways:

- When you are listing the qualities you have that you want to change, think of your Top Dog, Watch Dog, and Underdog and ask yourself: "What qualities do I most associate with each of them?" "How do I like those qualities in myself?" "Is there anything I want to get rid of or change?" These questions will help because you may overlook or not want to look at certain qualities in yourself. But looking at these three dogs will help you identify these otherwise overlooked or avoided qualities.

- When you are imagining yourself with the quality you want to develop, using the image of a dog you associate with that quality can help you focus more clearly on that quality and feel it more intensely. This focus is especially helpful in the case of qualities you want to develop, and thinking of the dog identified with that quality can serve as a trigger reminding you to express that quality. In effect, you are "Putting on the Dog", and choosing the particular dog to put on.

As you use the Transforming Unwanted into Wanted Qualities Chart, call on your dogs to help, think about the qualities you currently have but don't want and those you want to acquire.

TRANSFORMING UNWANTED INTO WANTED QUALITIES

Qualities I Don't Want to Have	Opposite or Different Qualities I Want to Have
1.	1.
2.	2.
3.	3.
4.	4.
5.	5.
6.	6.
7.	7.
8.	8.
9.	9.
10.	10.
11.	11.
12.	12.

Recognizing What or Who You Want to Become

Another way of changing your personality traits is through an intuitive holistic approach, where you use a process of mental scripting.

Say you have trouble being authoritative and feel uncomfortable being in charge, because you aren't sure people will follow your directions. Visualize yourself being more powerful and authoritative, and show more leadership in your position.

Or say you have difficulty controlling your temper with certain people or in certain situations, because you are overly sensitive and become angry when you feel disrespected or slighted. Imagine yourself controlling your anger and becoming a team player.

In the course of doing these visualizations, you can incorporate your chosen dogs, Guide Dogs, or Power Dogs to provide you with insights, advice, and support. For example, imagine one of your Power Dogs by your side as you give out directions and people follow you. Or see one of your Power Dogs jump in front of you to block the way to keep you from acting out your anger.

The following exercise will help you identify those characteristics you want to eliminate and those you want to adopt. After the exercise, you can use the Influencing the Personality Traits I Want to Change Chart to record your results.

Exercise: Identifying the Personality Traits You Want to Change

As you hold a copy of the Identifying the Personality Traits I Want to Change Chart before you, relax and close your eyes. Imagine one of your Guide Dogs is there to give you advice, and ask him or her: "What personality traits do I want to eliminate?" Be receptive and see what comes to you. As ideas or images come to mind, write them down on the chart in the first column. Don't try to judge whether you can get rid of that trait or not. Keep going until you have listed at least five traits or have started to slow down.

Then, ask your Guide Dog the question: "What difficult situations have I encountered in the past few weeks?" Again, be receptive and see what comes. As each scene appears in your mind, notice how you are acting and whether anything you are doing has been making this situation difficult for you. If so, this is probably a personality trait that you want to change. Write down this personality trait, too, in the first column. Keep going until you start to slow down.

Next, ask your Guide Dog the question: "What traits do I want to acquire?" In some cases, these traits may be the reverse of the traits you want to eliminate; in other cases, these may be different ones. Whatever comes to you is fine. Just list whatever comes up in the third column. Don't try to critique or evaluate the trait. And don't try to judge whether or not you can realistically acquire that trait. Again, keep going until you have listed at least five traits or have started to slow down.

Finally, ask you Guide Dog: "What new situations would I like to be in, where I am different than I am now?" Again be receptive and see what comes. As each scene appears, notice what personality traits you have that are making the situation feel very comfortable and natural. These may be personality qualities you want to acquire but don't have now. Write down in the third column any of these qualities that come up for you. Keep going until you start to slow down.

When you feel finished, you are ready to prioritize which traits you want to eliminate or develop first. To do so, look down the list of traits you want to eliminate; for each one, come up with the complementary or opposite trait you would like to acquire and list it in the second column (if you haven't already listed that trait in the third column). Ask your Guide Dog for advice on what should be most important or in your best interest if you aren't sure. Then, after you have listed this complementary trait or found it is *already in the third column, cross out the trait you want to eliminate from the first column.*

Now, look down the list of all the traits in columns two and three and prioritize them. To do so, rate each trait from 0 (low priority) to 3 (high priority), again asking your Guide Dog for advice to help you in making these ratings. Finally, look at the traits you have marked with the highest priority. Should you have more than one or two traits marked in this category, go through this list again and rank them again, until you have selected one or two traits that are the most important for you to work on. If there are two, note which is most important to you.

You have now established your priorities, so you can work on developing the quality that is most important to you. Should you have the time and energy, you can work on acquiring two qualities, but it's best not to work on more than two at a time. Once you feel solid about having made a particular trait or traits a part of your personality, you can go on to the next traits on your list in order of priority. Then, when you feel you have completed this process by incorporating these traits into your personality, you can make a new priority list for further changes.

IDENTIFYING THE PERSONALITY TRAITS I WANT TO CHANGE

Column 1	Column 2	Column 3	Column 4
Personality Traits I Want to Eliminate	Complementary Traits I Want to Acquire	Personality Traits I Want to Acquire	Priority Rating

Changing Your Overall Personality Orientation and Specific Traits

After you have identified the personality traits you want to change, you can work on changing your overall personality or your ability to change it under certain circumstances, or both, but don't try to change more than 2 or 3 things about yourself at a time. Remember, your overall personality traits, those associated with your Top Dog and Watch Dog, reflect your more general approach to relating to others and the world and reflect how you perceive information or make decisions. But you may express other personality traits and behavioral patterns, in response to a particular situation – the difference between the core you and your acting a role.

Using Mental Scripting to See Yourself As You Want to Be

Now that you have identified the personality traits to eliminate or acquire, you have a good baseline for thinking about what you want to change and who to become. You know the qualities to develop or eliminate and the specific traits to acquire. Now you can work on eliminating or acquiring these traits.

A good way to do this is through mental scripting to create new patterns and approaches in your mind that you can play out in everyday life.

How Mental Scripting Works

Mental scripting to develop or eliminate personality traits is much like the mental rehearsal technique to practice a particular skill or ability. However, in mental scripting, you create a more detailed scenario in which you mentally play out a desired role again and again until you create a habit pattern of action. As you repeatedly experience the action mentally, you reinforce the pattern in your mind. This process makes you feel increasingly certain you can play the role, and that confidence carries over into playing the scene in everyday life. You are like a movie director creating a scene for your own movie; you create the setting in which to play out your imagined script, where you possess the personality traits you desire. Meanwhile, your Guide Dogs or Power Dogs act as a team lending their support and cheering you on. It's like they are sitting beside the director's chair, and as you complete each phase of action, you can hear them bark and slap their paws on the ground to show that.

Perhaps you want to be more assertive and authoritative at work to advance your career. Picture yourself as more assertive and authoritative in your present position and see others respond to you in a more cooperative, agreeable way, acknowledging your desired leadership ability. You might see yourself giving instructions clearly and firmly, imagine others listening to you more seriously, and experience employees coming to you for advice. You might also project yourself into the future and see yourself expressing the desired leadership qualities in your new position as you sit in your new office, feeling very comfortable. Or imagine yourself doing the tasks you want to do, such as giving instructions to your staff, attending a board meeting, and flying to see an important client. In response, people defer to you and respect you in your new role. Meanwhile, as you do this visualization, you might imagine your Power Dogs are beside you giving you their support and power, so you feel even more calm, powerful, and self-assured.

The following exercise will help you create a mental script.

Exercise: Create a Mental Script to Be Who You Want to Be

Decide which trait you want to work on changing or acquiring. As before, get relaxed and close your eyes. Take a minute or two to focus on your breathing to get very calm and relaxed. Notice that one or more of your Power Dogs are beside you, lending you their strength and support for whatever you want to do.

Then, with that trait you want to change or acquire in mind, imagine a setting where you want to express that trait — at work, at home, with friends, anywhere. Tell yourself that you now have the trait you want to have, and see yourself expressing that trait in that setting. You are in the situation in which you have been, but now you are acting in this new way. See yourself vividly doing so. Notice the environment around you. Notice the colors, the people around you, the smells, the objects. Experience yourself interacting, talking with others. As you do, remind yourself that you have this quality you want to have, and you feel very comfortable, very natural, very confident, acting this new way. Meanwhile, your Power Dog is on the sidelines cheering you on. Experience this for a few minutes.

Now, project yourself into a future situation where you have this trait. It might be a move, a promotion, a new relationship. Whatever it is, tell yourself that you have this trait you want to have, and see yourself expressing it in this future setting. You see this future scene very clearly and vividly, as if it is happening now. Notice the environment around you. Notice the colors, the people around you, the smells, the objects. Experience yourself interacting, talking with others. As you do, remind yourself that you have this quality you want, and you feel very comfortable, very natural, very confident, acting this new way. Meanwhile, your Power Dog is on the sidelines cheering you on. Again, experience this for a few minutes.

When you feel ready, let go of the scene and let it fade. As it does, you feel very good, very confident, ready to put this new trait into practice in everyday life. Also, know that whenever you want to re-experience these feelings, this sense of assurance and confidence, you can think of your Power Dog, who has been here supporting you, and you will experience those feelings of assurance and confidence again.

Then, holding in your mind that feeling and enthusiasm to go out and act the way you want to be, return to the room. Count backward from 5 to 1, and as you do, you will come back. Five, four, becoming more and more alert. Three, two, almost back. And one. You are back in the room.

Practicing Your Mental Script

Once you have created a mental script you like, practice applying it in the real world. Practice a few minutes a day, until you really feel that new trait has become a part of you. Include the image of your Power Dog in the script, so when you call up that Power Dog association, you will feel that way, such as being more authoritative in the office, as noted before.

You may additionally want to replay a scene from your script, where you see yourself in this desired role. Then, should an appropriate situation arise when you want to be assertive, assert yourself and be firm. As you do, remember the feeling of confidence you felt as you asserted yourself in your mental script. And think of your Power Dog by your side, continuing to cheer you on and give you added support.

Similarly, if you imagined yourself being a more cooperative team player, go to work with this firm intention. Remind yourself that you are determined to be warmer, and friendly, and perhaps replay a scene from your script seeing yourself this way. Also see your Power Dog encouraging this warm, friendly behavior. Then, when at work, look for ways to express this intention, such as being friendlier than usual when you greet people. Or if you start to feel angry about something, think of the image of your friendly Power Dog and remind yourself that you are going to be cooperative and express yourself in a more gentle, accommodating way.

Turning Your Mental Script into Everyday Reality

Initially, when first working with mental scripts, you may have to pay extra attention to your script and repeatedly remind yourself that you are seeking to change by substituting a new way of feeling and acting. You may need to replay parts of your script from time to time and pay careful attention to what you say and do to break old patterns and replace them with new ways to act. You may also need to more consciously remind yourself that your Power Dog is ready to help you.

Eventually, though, as you keep inserting your new scripting into the way you act, it will become a habit, and after a while, you don't need to use the script anymore. The new trait and your behavior reflecting this trait will have become a part of you.

CHAPTER 2: TECHNIQUES TO UNDERSTAND AND IMPROVE YOUR RELATIONSHIPS

To better understand and improve your relationships with others, keep the basic personality, behavioral, and ethical styles in mind as you think about the people you know, want to know, or want to know better. Additionally, be familiar with the different types of dogs, which are organized in *What's Your Dog Type?* into 40 types or families of similar dogs. The more familiar you are with them, the more insights you can gain. Or choose a dog you are already familiar with that has a certain type of personality.

Maybe someone seems like a gentle, placid Collie, and you are very familiar with Collies, because someone down the block owns one. But as you learn more about the different dog types, you realize the person is more like the less familiar Chow Chow, because of his steadfast, quiet, reserved nature.

The following techniques illustrate how to use various visualization and reflection techniques to learn more about and improve your relationships. Since these exercises are designed to open up your ability to tap into your intuition, feel free to substitute quick "top-of-mind" impressions if you already get such insights. You'll also find that as you work with these techniques, you will increasingly get strong quick impressions, too.

Getting a Quick First Impression About the People You Meet

You can get a quick insight into someone when you first meet in two key ways:
- Through your immediate auditory or visual impressions when you first approach the person;

- Through your first impressions when you physically touch the person with a handshake or hug.

In both cases, you gain this insight by listening to your inner voice or noticing any spontaneous images that appear when you meet. This will give you clues about the person. While you can use any kinds of images to gain insights, using the different dog types, along with any other images, can help you develop an even clearer picture of that person. That's because you have already built up a series of associations with different dogs, so when that image appears, you immediately draw on those associations you already have. Any associations you have with other images are valuable clues; then the dog that comes to mind gives you another layer of associations and insight.

Suppose when you are introduced to a new business associate, you hear your inner voice say the word "tiger"; or suppose you see a tiger image briefly flash by in your mind's eye. Then, you see the image of a Great Dane, or hear your inner voice saying: "Great Dane." Those brief insights are significant. First, they suggest the person may have the characteristics you associate with a tiger, such as being wily, aggressive, and tenacious. Second, they suggest that the person has the characteristics associated with a Great Dane, such as being strong, powerful, and exercising leadership. So this is a person who likes to be dominant and in command, along with being crafty and clever. In dealing with this person, you can take these qualities into account.

Or suppose you only get a single image of a dog when you meet someone. That's fine, too. Just use your associations with that image, though you can seek additional images by saying to yourself: "What else do I think of when I see this person?" Then, let whatever image or images this question triggers come to mind, and think of your associations with that image or images.

This process of looking for images and associations may sound like a long process, and when you first start doing this, you generally need to consciously remind yourself to think of these dog and other images. But after a while, the process will become second nature, so these images will quickly come to mind when you first meet someone without you consciously directing the process.

Then, too, you can use the process to confirm or deepen your initial impressions on subsequent meetings. Say you picture the tiger and Great Dane at your first job interview. Then, the person calls you back for another interview. Notice if these same images come to mind or if you get other images. If so, these additional images can help you refine or add to your original image, or even correct your first impression. To illustrate, perhaps besides the tiger and Great Dane, you get an image of a small cat and a Collie. This might suggest that initially the person comes on as a strong, dominant, powerful person who wants to show leadership. However, he or she also has a warm, gentle, affectionate side when you get to know each other. In other words, the outer person is more like the tiger and Great Dane; the inner self is more like the cat and Collie. Another way to think of these contrasting personality images and personality traits is that the Great Dane is like the person's Top Dog, the Collie like their Watch Dog. This distinction is comparable to what the Myers-Brigg's system refers to as the Superior and Inferior Functions, or the birth sign and the rising sign in astrology.

The following exercises will help you become more aware of your first impressions and your accuracy, so you can feel more confident of your abilities. Over time, your sensitivity to others will increase as you practice paying more attention to your initial responses.

In doing these exercises, carry a small pad or notebook to jot down your impressions when you first observe or meet someone, though, make these notes discreetly. If you're in a class or meeting, where you can take notes on the spot, fine. If not, find a place to make your notes unobserved as soon as possible after your observations.

When you get to know the person better or learn about him or her from others, compare your initial impressions with what you learn later. You'll find you are quite accurate and that your accuracy increases with practice.

There are three types of initial impressions to observe: (1) when you first see someone; (2) when you first meet someone; and (3) when you make an initial physical contact by shaking hands. The following exercises illustrate how to do this.

Getting First Impressions

- Get Impressions When You First See Someone. *This technique is ideal for when you go to an event and see someone you expect to talk to or meet later. Or use it at a meeting when you first arrive. Look in turn at each person you want to know about, and think of the first word or picture that comes to mind along with the first dog you think of. Write these images down as soon as you can and think what that word or picture and dog mean to you. That will give you a general impression of the person. After you meet the person, review your comments to see how accurate you were — and watch your accuracy increase as you continue to do this.*
- Get Impressions When You First Meet Someone. *This technique is ideal for a gathering where you can meet someone or observe that person meeting and talking with others. As you walk up to meet the person, be aware of the type of dog and any other words or images that pop up when the person speaks to a group or meets another person. Write down these words and images as soon as you can and think about what they mean. Later, as you get to know this person or see him or her in action, review your comments to check your level of accuracy.*
- Get Impressions When You Make Initial Physical Contact by Shaking Hands. *This technique is ideal whenever you shake hands with someone you meet and expect to engage in further conversation. While you shake hands, focus your awareness on that handshake, and notice what dog and any other words or images appear in your mind's eye. Ask*

yourself what they mean to you, and if you continue to converse, check your accuracy. How much did this first impression tell you about the person? And how consistent is this impression with what you sense or learn from the person as you talk? Again, you'll find your accuracy goes up with practice.

Getting Advance Impressions of Someone Before You Meet

When you are about to meet someone you don't know for whatever reason, some advance insight about this person's personality type can help you act so the meeting goes more smoothly.

The personality types and behavioral styles described earlier will give you the framework for organizing the insights you receive. It is also helpful to review any preliminary information you have about the person, including name, nickname, occupational title, photograph, or organizations the person belongs to.

Once you have this information in mind, you are ready to perform this technique.

Get relaxed, close your eyes, and call up an image or the name of the person you are going to meet in your mind's eye. Concentrate on making this image or name expand and contract for about one minute. Next, see the image form into a white ball of energy, and watch that energy swirl around and form into a computer screen. On that screen, you first see the image of a dog appear. Next a word appears that describes the person as a take-charge personality, an analyzer/explorer, a people person, or a conscientious planner. Should you see two dogs or two or more names appear simultaneously, the person is a combination of these primary types.

Then, with an image of that dog and that word in mind, think of the traits you associate with that image and word. Now with this image, word, and associated traits in mind, see yourself meeting this person for the first time. As you do, notice what you say and how you act.

Later, when you meet the person, this mental rehearsal will help you make a good impression and relate to the person from his or her perspective.

Gaining In-Depth Insight into Others

After you have met someone and have an ongoing relationship, these in-depth techniques can help you gain additional insights about the person or further your relationship. At work, these methods can help to promote smoother relationships with co-workers, manage a work team more effectively, or influence an employer to regard you more favorably. In a personal relationship, these can help you have a closer, more loving relationship with a partner and get along better with friends and family.

These techniques work by focusing your intuitive abilities on reading the individual's personality in more depth than an initial impression. As such, they are much like the techniques used by professionals who do a personality reading on someone desiring spiritual or psychic counseling. But everyone has these intuitive abilities. The more you practice with them, the more accurate and detailed information you will get.

The basic approach is to use an object, imagery or new way of seeing to perceive information about someone. You gain this information intuitively by calling up images of the person's past, body, thoughts, or surrounding energy field and the dog you associate with that person. The person can be physically present or not. If he or she isn't present, just visualize him or her in front of you.

Besides using the images of dogs, you can use any other images and even create your own symbol system. Any imagery system will work if you get used to using it. To become more accurate, try reading some people you don't know well; then ask for feedback to check your accuracy. If you're off at first, don't worry. Your accuracy will improve with practice, along with your confidence.

Get relaxed for all of these techniques, and except for the aura reading technique, close your eyes. Preferably, sit upright in a receptive position.

Using Objects to Learn About Others

Using objects to gain information about others is a technique, often called "Psychometry," that involves getting associations from an object a person owns. You hold the object and think about the images and associations that come to you. Sometimes people do this technique by just looking at a portion of an object. Here's a guide you can use for this technique.

To begin, ask someone for a small object. Then, with the person present or at a later time, hold this object in your hand and meditate on it. See it in your mind's eye. Try touching it to your forehead. Notice what dog and what other words, images, or impressions appear, and think about the associations you have with that dog and the other words, images, or impressions you experience.

Say your thoughts aloud if the person is present, such as in a workshop or one-on-one exchange. Write them down if you like. And if the person isn't present, record what you experience.

These impressions can provide clues to the person's personality, interests, relationships, and life style. If possible, share your impressions with your subject and get feedback. Alternatively, pay attention to how this person interacts with you and others to see how well you have done in assessing what this person is like.

As with other techniques, your accuracy will improve over time as you continue to work with this technique and become increasingly familiar with the dog types and the characteristics associated with each type.

Learning About a Person from His or Her Energy Centers

This energy center technique draws on the principles of many holistic health and spiritual traditions, which state that each person has a series of energy concentrations or centers in the body, located from the base of the spine to the top of the head. These centers, sometimes called "chakras" (a term borrowed from the Hindus and Buddhists), can provide a window into a person's inner self, because the personality is reflected by the flow of energy through the body.

There are seven primary centers, each linked with a different personal quality. These are:

1. The base of the spine – survival
2. The reproductive area – sexual energy
3. The stomach or solar plexus – identity, will
4. The heart – warmth and emotions
5. The throat – communication
6. The center of the forehead (third eye) – perception
7. The top of the head (crown charka) - spirituality

To read someone's energy centers, call on the help of a Guide Dog or Top Dog who will act as your counselor and advisor. To begin, sit in front of the person you will be reading or visualize him or her before you. After you relax and close your eyes, visualize as follows:

First, call on your Guide Dog or Top Dog to help you. See this dog sitting beside you, giving you support and advice.

In this process, you'll imagine a rose in front of each energy center in turn, and you'll also see what dog comes to mind at each of these centers.

First, see the petals or the whole rose and stem. Then, notice that your Guide Dog or Top Dog is especially interested in this rose. He looks at it closely, and perhaps goes to sniff it, to really feel a close connection with this rose.

Now starting at the base of the spine, place an image of the rose in front of this energy center. Observe what happens to the rose. Ask your Guide Dog or Top Dog to give you advice as you observe and ask a series of questions. These are: What type of dog is next to the rose? Does the rose change color or shape? Does it begin to move? Does it assume the shape of an animal or person? Does anything else happen to it? Let the impressions come spontaneously, and don't try to analyze. Say them aloud or write them down, as you wish.

Once these images stop coming, ask yourself what they mean in light of the characteristics associated with the first lower energy center. Notice what impressions or explanations spontaneously come, and jot them down.

Now go up to the next energy center and observe what type of dog is next to rose. Again, notice what happens to the rose and ask what this means.

Keep doing this process until you conclude with the energy center at the top of the head.

In performing this exercise, be aware there is no fixed meaning for any image, although there are some general associations with each type of dog. What's most important is what the images or symbols mean to you, as every person is different and has a different symbol system. Also, an image means different things depending on which energy center it is associated with.

For example, say you are focusing on the lowest energy center at the base of the spine, which is associated with survival. Suddenly, the image of a Pit Bull appears, and then a rose opens up and becomes very bright. These images suggest that the person is very ambitious, because he or she is acting strongly in the area of survival (suggested by the bright open rose), and is willing to aggressively go after what he wants (suggested by the Pit Bull). In fact, more than being just aggressive, the person may be willing to fight with great tenacity, much like a Pit Bull trained to fight.

By contrast, if these same images appear in front of the heart center, it may suggest the person is very warm and emotional (the rose), and even impulsive and quick to respond (the Pit Bull), as his or her heart opens up.

Learning about a Person's Past or Future

You can read someone's present and past, whether that person is with you or not. You simply see this person before you in your mind's eye and, you call on your Guide Dog or Top Dog to act as your counselor or advisor. In either case, use the following scenario as a guide.

Now, on your mental screen, see yourself going into a large library with your Guide Dog or Top Dog.

A large marble stairway is before you. You go up the stairs, your dog beside you. At the top you see a door with a sign that says, "Reference". You go in with your dog and enter a large room, which has many long tables and files.

You walk toward a series of large file drawers in the center of the room. There are some letters on each file, and you look for the drawer with the letter corresponding to the name of your subject. When you find it, pull out this drawer and flip through the cards. Invite your Guide Dog or Top Dog to help you look, perhaps by sniffing as you flip through the files for the scent of the person you are seeking information about.

Finally, you come to that person's name, pull out his or her card, and noticed a date on the top right hand corner. Look at it. It designates a period in this person's life in the past, present, or future. To learn what happened or will happen, look at the center of the card. A biography is written there. Read it and learn what you want to know.

After you read the card, put it back. If you wish, pull out another card and read it, too.

When you are ready, leave the library with your Guide Dog or Top Dog. Go down the same marble stairs, and when you return to the street, return to normal consciousness.

As a variation on this technique, enter the library with a time period in mind and find a card with that date. Visualize the cards arranged in a time sequence, and flip through the cards until you find the right date.

After you complete the reading, record your impressions to better remember them. Later, get feedback when you can to test your perception. If you can't ask your subject directly, say because you don't feel comfortable telling your boss, "I've been trying to learn about you intuitively", try to bring up the topic in the course of conversation. You'll find your accuracy improves over time, and even if some specific details are wrong, you'll find your overall impression is correct. (For instance, you get an image of a friend as a boxing champ as a teen, whereas he fought to protect himself from neighborhood gangs.)

You can use these insights to help you build a better relationship with this person. For instance, some insights might suggest topics of conversation to improve your rapport. (Say you sense the person has been a scrappy fighter since childhood; you might comment on a recent newspaper article about a whistle blower or someone who foiled an attempted robbery).

These insights might also give you guidance in how to better relate to that person. Say you get an image of the person as an adventurous traveler and outdoors person. If that person is a friend, that might suggest not only talking about travel and outdoors activities, but going on a trip with this person. Or if you are that person's employer, that might suggest giving the person additional challenges to solve, since this is someone eager to face down hard challenges.

Increasing Understanding Through Identification

Another way to gain information about someone to improve your relationship is by using visualization to identify with that person and by using a guide, such as your Guide Dog or Top Dog to ask questions of yourself as this person. One approach, featured in the following exercise, is to imagine yourself putting on another person's head and responding as he or she would, as your Guide Dog or Top Dog asks questions and gives advice. Use the following guide to experience this.

To begin, close your eyes and get relaxed. See your Guide Dog or Top Dog seated beside you, ready to help you ask questions and give you advice.

Now visualize the person you want to know more about standing in front of you. Observe his or her face carefully. Notice the eyes, lips, and facial features. Look at how he or she smiles. Next, stretch out your arms and lift his head from his body and place it on yours. As you do, your Guide Dog or Top Dog sits beside you watching.

Now look around and experience how the world looks through this other person's eyes. What do you see? Hear? Feel?

Now invite your Guide Dog or Top Dog to ask you questions about your new self or ask some questions yourself. Ask about whatever you want to know. Depending on who's asking, ask the question as "You" or "I" questions. For instance, your Guide Dog might ask: "What do you like to do?" "Where did you live as a child?" "What kind of work do you do?" Or you might ask: "What do I like to do?" and so on.

> *Don't try to answer consciously. Just let the answers pop into your mind. Then, say your answers aloud or write them down.*
>
> *Now, start asking your questions for a minute or two.*
>
> *After you finish your questions, take the head off and put it back on the person's body. Then, thank your Guide Dog or Top Dog for his or her help, return to normal consciousness, and open your eyes.*

Later, if you can, get feedback directly or during an ordinary conversation from this person to check your accuracy. With practice, your ability will improve.

Taking a Visual Visit

Another way to gain information is to project your consciousness outside your body and imagine visiting a person's house. While you can visit on your own, you can get additional insights by taking your Guide Dog or Top Dog with you, to get their opinions and advice. The way the house looks in your imagination, whether accurate or not, and your associations with that house, will tell you something about what that person is like.

> *To begin, imagine your Guide Dog or Top Dig is beside you, eager to help and give you information. Now visualize the person you want to visit. It can be someone you know or not.*
>
> *Then, see yourself leaving your body in a rush of energy, which rises from the base of your spine, spirals up, and goes out through your head. This energy continues to rise, lifting your inner self with it, until you come up to a soft, white cloud floating by. You get off onto the cloud, and for a few minutes, you float, feeling completely peaceful, calm, and free.*

Then, as you relax on this cloud, your Guide Dog or Top Dog comes over to you to act as your advisor and counselor.

Now it is time to descend for your visit. Float down off your cloud with your Guide Dog or Top Dog beside you. Below you, see this person's house. Note what it looks like. Observe the surroundings. Ask your Guide Dog or Top Dog what he or she thinks about the house and the type of person who might live there.

Then, float in through the door with your Guide Dog or Top Dog following right behind you. If anyone is there, do not talk to him. Just observe. What is the interior like? How many rooms? How large? What shape? How about the furnishings? Are there any animals or plants? Who else lives here besides this person? Notice, too, what type of dog comes to mind when you characterize this person or any other people living there.

Then ask yourself or your Guide Dog or Top Dog what each image tells you about this person.

When you finish reviewing the images, return to your cloud with your Guide Dog or Top Dog and float back to where you first got off. Then, spiral down, and let your energy and consciousness return to your head.

After your experience, record any details. Later, if possible, get feedback from the person you visited to check your accuracy. How accurately did you perceive his or her house? More importantly, how accurate were you in describing the characteristics of this person from your observations?

Using Energy Fields to Learn More About People

Another source of information is the electro-magnetic energy field around each person, which is often called the "aura". Some research has suggested this is a real physical field, because Kirlian photography has been used to photograph the radiant heat surrounding the physical body. If you prefer, think of it as a radiating energy capsule surrounding the body.

Depending on a person's state of mind, mood, and personality and your perceptions of the person, you will see this field expand, contract, or change color. As you gaze steadily ahead, your eyes out of focus, you will normally be able to see or sense this aura, and obtain information about the person from it. While you can use this technique on its own, as described in *Mind Power*, you can gain additional information with the help of your Guide Dogs or Top Dog and by noticing any dog images that appear in this energy field.

A Quick Introduction to the Aura

If you aren't already familiar with energy fields or auras, here are a few general characteristics, so you will understand what you see. An aura usually looks like a light filmy after-image surrounding each person. It tends to expand when a person is positive, healthy, active, assertive, or thinks of power; and to contract when one is negative, ill, passive, withdrawn, or thinks of weakness. It frequently appears with colors — usually light, fuzzy, pastel tones — and these colors express a person's personality traits.

One observer may perceive these images of the aura differently from another, since each person is different, and the observer-subject interaction differs in each case. However, certain color associations are common, though the associations may vary in different countries and cultures. The common associations in the West are:

- Red - energy power, courage, strength, love, warmth
- Yellow – intellect, thought
- Orange – sexuality, activity, job
- Green – health, healing, spiritual growth
- Blue – peace, calm, spirituality, coolness
- Purple – royalty, mysticism, spiritual truth

- White – purity, spiritual attainment
- Gray, Black – sadness, depression, illness

In addition to colors, you may notice that the image of one or more dogs appear in the person's energy field in various forms, such as standing close to the person or superimposed on the persons' head. When you do, add your associations with the dog or dogs to your interpretation of the person's energy field.

Observing the Aura

Now, use the following guide to help direct your attention, start observing the aura and interpreting what you see.

To see the aura, look at the person in an unfocused way, as if you're staring into the distance. Then, keep looking. The aura will emerge as a frame of light and color around the person. Usually it will appear around his or her head first as a white shimmer of energy, then it may encircle the whole body. At first, you may see only white. But as you practice, colors should appear, usually with a fuzzy, pastel quality.

In time, you can see auras under any condition. Just look, and they will appear. You may even be able to see them by just imagining that the person is in front of you. As you concentrate on the person in your imagination, you will gradually see an aura emerge, just as you would if the person is there. This ability takes a little longer to develop, but many people can do this.

To facilitate seeing these auras initially, practice under optimal conditions: in a quiet place with dim lighting. Ideally, have your subject (perhaps a friend you are practicing with] sit against a large white or softly colored wall. Imagine that your Guide Dog or Top Dog is with you as a counselor and advisor.

Then, stare at the center of the person's forehead for a few minutes. Watch for a fuzzy whiteness to appear around *the head. This is the aura. Gradually it may grow larger and brighter. It may vary in size and intensity around different parts of the body. Soft colors may emerge, too.*

As you continue looking, you may see the image of a dog beside the person, or you may see its head imposed on the person. Notice what breed or type of dog this is. Later you can interpret the meaning of the colors and the type of dog you have seen.

Once the aura and any dog image emerge, shift your eyes to observe the aura around different parts of the body. But keep your awareness unfocused. Should the aura begin to fade, look back at the subject's forehead, until you see the aura's strength return.

After several minutes of looking, ask your Guide Dog or Top Dog what these colors and images mean and listen for the answers. Don't try to direct these responses – just be receptive and listen.

Next share your observations and initial interpretations with your subject, and add any additional interpretations of what you have seen. Again, seek feedback about your accuracy to help you improve.

Two Aura Exercises to Develop Your Ability to See Auras

To further develop your ability to see auras, try these aura exercises with a friend. One of you should meditate on some idea or image to affect your aura, while the other observes. Then, the observer compares his or her perceptions with what the mediator was doing. While you can look at auras on your own, you can gain additional insights by imagining your Guide Dog or Top Dog is sitting beside you as a counselor and advisor, who asks questions or gives suggestions about what you are seeing. You'll be amazed at your accuracy. Three experiments to try are:

- One person concentrates on an image of power or weakness to expand or contract the aura, while the other observes.
- One person concentrates on sending his or her energy to the left or right, while the other observes.
- One person concentrates on imagining different types of dogs on either side, or imagines putting their heads over his or her head, while the other observes.

How to Apply Insights Gained from the Aura

Once you are sensitive to perceiving the aura and understanding what it tells you about the person, you can apply this information on an ongoing basis to build a better relationship. Improving a relationship can be especially useful in a business setting to better build rapport with those you work with or for better relating to clients and customers. Or use the insights of aura reading with friends and family members to gain a greater closeness and better get along on a day to day basis.

Gaining a better relationship from aura reading can occur because reading a person's aura can make you more sensitive to everyday mood swings, so you can react appropriately. For instance, say you approach your boss to ask for a raise and you notice a great deal of red and gray in his aura, along with the image of a Jack Russell Terrier. The colors suggest a mixture of anger and sadness, while the Terrier suggests a willingness to fight if provoked, although outwardly your boss appears calm and impassive as usual. This insight tells you that may not be the best time to seek a raise; rather you may do better if you wait until you sense that his aura has more positive colors, such as red, along with yellow, orange, or green, suggesting power, warmth, happiness, and health.

Similarly, if you are negotiating with someone, you might pick up information from the aura about the person's relative strength or willingness to give in or compromise. For instance, if you see lots of reds in the aura along with the image of a Bulldog, that suggests that the person is not only feeling strong and powerful, but may be determined to stick to whatever position he first embraces. Thus, you know you must strengthen your own position to prevail and you may have to be especially forceful and convincing. But if you see yellows and the image of a different, more docile dog – say a Labrador Retriever, this suggests the person is becoming more thoughtful and may be ready to compromise. Should you see blues or dark colors or the image of a small, usually yielding dog – say a Chinese Crested, the person may be willing to concede, and it's time to press toward a close.

In short, you can use information from an aura reading to supplement the other more visible cues a person is giving off through body language, gestures, facial cues, words, and eye movements.

Using Visualization and Dog Profiling Techniques to Improve Your Relationships

Besides gaining insights and information, you can use visualization techniques to directly affect your relationships. One way is to make people feel better about the relationship by chasing away any negative, angry feelings or by emphasizing warm, supportive, loving feelings. Another way is reinforcing your feelings of power and making others more aware you have this power.

The basic process involves setting your goal for the relationship. Then, focus your mental energy on this other person as you visualize your goal and mentally send a message about this to the person. You can gain even more strength in the process by calling on your Power Dogs or Top Dog to contribute their support and strength.

This process works on two levels. First, it helps you change your attitude toward the person, so when you see each other again, you will interact in light of your desired goal, which will influence the other person to respond accordingly.

Secondly, since thoughts have energy, as shown by some research in which monkeys have directed a computer cursor with their thoughts, the person to whom you direct this thought transmission will receive it on an inner neural, psychic, or mental level. Consciously he or she may not be aware of your message. But your mental communication may inspire or remind him or her to relate to you in this desired way.

One common use of this visualization approach is smoothing the way for a future meeting with someone. Also, some people use this method to send their thoughts to encourage someone to get in touch with them.

The following exercises will help you to improve your relationships with these techniques in various ways.

Creating a Warmer Relationship

To overcome angry feelings, resentments, misunderstandings, or make someone feel warm, friendly and positive toward you, send a little love someone's way. You can call on one of your Power Dogs or Top Dog to help send it.

Sending love will help eliminate any negative feelings and make you feel good. This process can be especially helpful after an argument with someone, since your positive thoughts can reduce or eliminate any remaining hard feelings, so when you see each other again, the conflict may be gone. Sending love can also make someone who is distant from you in reality or is just reserved become closer. For instance, if someone is in another country, this technique is ideal for giving a supportive energy boost.

The first exercise involves sending love to prepare the way for a better meeting. The second is designed to send love and persuade someone to contact you.

- **Sending Love**

    Put up a picture of the person to whom you're sending love before you and imagine a glowing ball of love radiating out from your heart to this person. At the same time, imagine that your Power Dog or Top Dog is seated beside you sending these warm vibrations of love and concern, too.

As you send out this beam of energy, say the word "love" over and over to yourself, and send these words along this beam. Notice that your Power Dog or Top Dog is sending out this love energy, too, perhaps barking happily and enthusiastically or just radiating this warm light.

As this beam arrives, notice that the person begins to glow and radiates love back. You may even see the person's Top Dog beside him, basking in the warmth of this beam of love you are sending.

Continue to focus on this image for several minutes. Notice how it becomes more and more brilliant as you continue sending love.

Now visualize the next meeting you expect to have with this person. See the setting as vividly as possible. Notice whatever is around you, imagine what the person is wearing and doing. As you approach, with your Power Dog or Top Dog still beside you, continue to feel these warm, friendly feelings, and notice that the other person responds the same way. If you have felt any anger or resentments toward each other, that is gone.

After this initial meeting, you can continue your conversation with this person and notice that you now have a better rapport. When you conclude the conversation, you feel satisfied that you have achieved your goal of a warmer, more comfortable relationship together.

Later, when you see this person in reality, notice that you feel more open and warmer when you meet, which will contribute to creating better rapport with each other.

- **Promoting Communication**

To get someone to contact you or be more receptive to a call from you, visualize sending this person a message. Use your Power Dog or Top Dog to put even more energy into sending out this message.

If you feel there has been any problem in the relationship to overcome (such as an argument or feelings of resentment), or if you want to make the relationship warmer, start by sending love as in the previous exercise. Then, use the following mind to mind communication technique to promote the desired contact.

> *Take a few minutes about the same time each day to get relaxed in a quiet place. Then, visualize your Power Dog or Top Dog beside you, and see the person you want to communicate with in your mind's eye. Now mentally ask him or her to contact you or be receptive to your call by imagining a cable of pure white energy radiating from your mind to this person with your message. Also, see the energy of your Power Dog or Top Dog going into this message, making it even stronger. Imagine that this beam of energy continues to transmit your request with all this energy invested in it for about 2-3 minutes. Then, see this person contacting you by phone, letter, e-mail, or in person — however you wish to receive the message, or being receptive to you when you initiate contact.*
>
> *Do this visualization regularly for several days, and frequently, you'll find the person will call. Or if the person hasn't, feel confident you have paved the way for a successful call when you call yourself. Then, get ready to make your call, feeling infused by all the energy you and your Power Dog or Top Dog have sent out to prepare the way.*

- **Promoting a Closer Relationship**

Another way to promote a closer relationship or to get someone to contact you is by using an object representing you and the other person, such as a candle, to help you focus and reinforce your message. This technique has frequently been used to impress a love relationship, but you can also use it to promote friendships and closer understandings with the people you work with. In addition, to increase the energy you are sending out, imagine your Power Dog or Top Dog beside you, sending out energy, too.

As in the previous exercise for Promoting Communication, take a few minutes each day for several days to go through this process until your message starts having its effect. The following example uses candles as the object, but you can use whatever you feel most comfortable with, such as small figurines, statues, or even chess and other game pieces, to represent you and the other person.

To prepare, get two candles, one representing you and the other the person you want to hear from. (For example, pink and blue candles might be used for a woman and man respectively, although any colors with personal meaning are fine.) The first day you do this technique, set the candles about twelve inches apart. On each successive day, begin by placing the candles two inches closer together, until on the seventh day, they touch. Thereafter, leave the candles touching.

Now light the candles and turn off any lights. Imagine your Power Dog or Top Dog is by your side as you do this, sending you even more energy and power.

Look back and forth from one candle to another for about one minute. Then, close your eyes and see the candles burning in your mind's eye. Next see the two flames draw together, until they become a single flame. Observe the bright yellow beam that radiates from this flame.

Now put one hand around the base of each candle, as you imagine your Power Dog or Top Dog seated beside you, sending you its energy. Continue to hold your hands there, while you visualize this beam traveling across space and time to the person you want to contact you. Continue to hold these candles and concentrate on this image for 2-3 minutes. Then, gently, push each candle about an inch toward the other (or once they are together, press them together tightly). As you do this, think to yourself: "We are drawing closer and closer together. We are drawing closer and closer together. May he (she) contact me. (Or be receptive to my call.)" Or express these sentiments in your own words.

When you feel the message has been sent, let go of the candles, return to normal consciousness, and open your eyes.

After you finish the exercise, leave the candles in position, if you plan to do this technique again.

Do this exercise regularly for about a week, and expect your call. Quite frequently, the person will have called you by then. If not, feel confident your call will be successful and contact the person yourself. When you do, feel infused by the positive energy you have generated with the help of your Power Dog or Top Dog to prepare the way.

Increasing Your Power in a Relationship

To increase your power balance in a relationship, use the same principle as in the techniques to create warmer feelings. Here you'll visualize a mental scenario in which you experience yourself being powerful, and you call on your Power Dog or other dog you think of as very powerful to make you feel more powerful. Then, you imagine yourself in a likely scene with this person, in which you express this newly felt sense of power.

The following is a sample scenario you can use to increase your feelings of power.

Put up a picture of the person with whom you want to experience your greater power, and see the image of your Power Dog or any other dog you consider very powerful before you. Additionally, call on other images of power to surround you, such as a powerful animal like a lion, a powerful vehicle like a rocket ship, a powerful person like a weight lifter or body builder.

Concentrate on seeing these images of power vividly inから of and around you, and feel the power that radiates from these images.

Then, direct a beam of your energy from your power center in your stomach area to this person. Feel the energy from your Power Dog and other dogs infusing you with their power, like recharging a battery. At the same time, say the word "power" over and over to yourself, and send these words along this beam. Notice that you are feeling more and more powerful as you do, and notice that the person you want to impress is also aware of this. Continue to focus on this beam of powerful energy surging from you for several moments, and notice that it becomes stronger and stronger as you continue to beam your power into this image.

Now visualize the next meeting you expect to have with this person. See the setting as vividly as possible. Notice whatever is around you. Imagine what the person is wearing and doing. As you approach, continue to feel these strong, powerful feelings, and notice that the other person responds accordingly. He or she regards you with increased respect, is more deferential, is more willing to listen to you. Notice, too, that any feelings of uncertainty you may have felt are completely gone, and you feel confident and sure of yourself.

Once you meet, continue your conversation, and continue to relate to this person from your power place. When you conclude the conversation, you feel satisfied that you have achieved your goal of having and exuding more power when you interact with this person in the future.

Later, when you see this person in reality, notice that you feel much more confident and powerful, which will contribute to the person treating you with more seriousness and respect.

Influencing Your Relationships in Other Ways

You'll find that using these visualization techniques with the help of your Guide Dogs, Power Dogs, and Top Dog will improve your relationships, either by changing the way you relate or by modifying how others perceive and respond to you.

While many people are especially interested in improving the emotional tone or power balance in a relationship, you can create other techniques to influence your relationships in other ways. To do so, create a visualization that expresses your goal in a relationship. Then, call on your Guide Dogs for advice or insights or call on your Power Dogs to increase your power. Call on your Top Dog for either kind of help.

For instance, say you want to take more initiative or responsibility in the relationship, and you want the other person to give you more space or trust, so you can do this (as might be the case when an employee wants to expand his job responsibilities or when a partner in a relationship wants to become more assertive). To gain this increased initiative or responsibility, create a visualization with an image of doing something when you take initiative or responsibility. You can use the image of a dog you associate with these qualities, such as a St. Bernard or Bernese Mountain Dog, or choose another animal with those characteristics, such as a fox. Then, direct your beam of energy into that image, and see yourself interacting with the person in this way.

Or say you want more freedom and independence (perhaps to set your own hours and schedule). Create an image that suggests freedom or independence to you (such as visualizing a dog like a Siberian Husky or a free-ranging animal like a bird or tiger).Then, beam yourself into that and imagine you are interacting with the person, while holding that image in mind.

In short, make these exercises your own by using symbols with meaning for you, as well as calling on the dogs that feel most supportive. You'll find that your relationships change dramatically in the direction you want. One reason is that these exercises will help change you, as you clarify what you want and focus your energy toward achieving your goal. At the same time, the energy you send may contribute to changing the other person, for the same reason that the thoughts of a monkey can impact the movements of a cursor on a computer. As researchers are finding, there is something very real about these mental energies, so by visualizing what you want and pouring your energy into that, you have a real impact on others.

So whether you want more warmth, rapport, or power in your relationships, or want to influence your relationships in other ways, use visualization to help you shape what you want. At the same time, call on your Guide Dogs, Power Dogs, or Top Dog to help guide your visualizations and provide you with even more energy and power to shape what you want.

CHAPTER 3: A WORKSHOP ON WORKING WITH YOUR GUIDE DOG

Discovering Your Dog Type included a workshop in which people discovered and contacted their Top Dog, Watch Dog, and Underdog to show how people could gain insights about themselves for personal and professional development.

You can similarly hold a workshop to show how the Dog Type system can be used to better understand others, improve relationships, and deal with everyday issues and problems. Here are highlights from a workshop I conducted on working with your Guide Dog.

The Workshop Setting

After a brief introduction to the Dog Type system and the Top Dog, Watch Dog, Underdog, Guide Dogs, and Power Dogs, I invited participants to say a little about themselves and what they hoped to gain from the workshop. This time the participants included Andrea, a financial adviser; David, an interviewer for a marketing company; Ellen, a city clerk; Paul, a salesman; Frank, an investment broker; and Sharon, a social service agency supervisor.

Andrea, who owned a Rottweiler, was particularly interested in knowing how people with the traits of different dogs interacted with others. Plus, she was curious in mingling with other dog owners and about the odd disparity that sometimes occurred between the personality of a dog owner and their dog, though their personalities matched.

Why? I explained it's a little like choosing a mate:

"You are often drawn to a dog that is similar to you in personality, but at times you may be drawn to one that has traits that complement your own or has traits that you'd like to develop yourself. That's much like how people choose mates – either they have similar characteristics that echo them or they have complementary qualities they don't have. For instance, an energetic person may be drawn to a laid back person, because one is relaxed by the other, while the other person gets energized. Or somebody who's very quiet and introverted may be drawn to somebody who's very outgoing, so they balance each other."

Then, David wondered why he chose mixed breeds as did most of the people he knew.

"Then, if you feel one breed doesn't quite fit you, your Top Dog might be a mixture of two types of dogs." I explained.

For Ellen, the big question was personality differences that led to clashes between people and between dogs. "What if you get a dog that's different from you in personality? Does the dog adapt to you, or do you adapt to the dog?" And what if you have a relationship with someone and you're different as night and day, too? What do you do? How do you work things out?"

"There could be a compromise, or if you recognize you are in a dysfunctional relationship, you might think about how you might change it to create a more successful relationship. Or if that isn't possible, you might leave it and move on. Consider the possibilities and decide what works best for you," I told her.

Meeting One's Guide Dog (or Dogs)

While it is possible to achieve these insights directly by thinking of the first association that comes to mind when you meet someone, I used the guided visualization described in Chapter 4 in which people go to a pet store and see many dogs from which they choose their Guide Dog. I also provided a brief introduction to set the stage for this exercise:

"I'd like to begin by having you meet your inner Guide Dog. You can have one or more of these. Your Guide Dog can be the same as your Top Dog or Watch Dog or a totally different dog. It plays the role of a teacher, helper, or wise person. You might compare Guide Dogs to spiritual teachers, guides, angels, or other helpers that people call on for help on a visual plane.

In this exercise, you'll imagine you are going to a Pet Store, where you will find your Guide Dog."

After the exercise, I asked everyone to talk about what type of dog they chose and why. Some of the key reasons were seeing a dog as a protector; intelligent, confident, wise teacher, or just a fun companion. In some cases, the participants drew on an experience where their own dogs had acted as helpers and guides in various situations, such as protecting them from danger or steering them away from unpleasant people.

Andrea said she chose a German Shepherd because "He's very sensitive. I saw him as very strong and protective, and I feel I need that now."

Ellen explained that she chose a Collie, because she found him playful as well as protective.

"I'm at a time in my life, when I want to relax and enjoy whatever I'm doing, since I feel I've been working too hard, and I live in a fairly tough neighborhood, where there's a lot of crime and drug dealers. So a Collie seemed just perfect for me. I can play with it and be protected by it."

David chose two dogs and he used his real-life knowledge of different dogs to decide to call on as a personal Guide Dog. As he explained:

"I ended up with two very different dogs. One was an Alaskan Sled dog, a huge, dog, who's very confident and in control. The other one was a Border Collie, which is like a cattle dog, very intelligent. For example, when I've seen them play with other dogs, I've seen them run in circles around them and gather them into a group, like they are herding the other dogs. Now that's pretty smart, I think."

When David wondered why he had chosen two very different dogs, I explained he could use them for very different kinds of advice. "Consider them like a team of dogs. You can always add more Guide Dogs to the team that you can call on for different purposes."

Getting Help from One's Guide Dogs

After the participants selected their Guide Dogs, who they could ask for advice, I took them on a "Dog Walk", using the exercise described in Chapter 4.

After the exercise, we discussed what people experienced and how they had gotten help from their Guide Dog. Here are some highlights of what people experienced.

Frank found he had three Guide Dogs who helped him, explaining:

"I had three dogs that joined me – one was my dog in reality, and two other dogs who came to help him. I found my dog really helpful and wise, since he always seems to know the way. For instance, he guides me through the urban forests when I take him on a walk, and it's like following a trail in the woods. He starts to smell which way to go, and I've had a lot of dreams in which he has guided me through problems. So, he was there by my side with these two other dogs."

For Sharon, her Guide Dog provided some reassurance that everything would turn out all right. She felt she especially needed such support now, since she had recently lost her job due to the economic downturn and city budget cuts, and she was unsure whether to stay in the social service field or seek other types of training and jobs. As Sharon explained:

"My Guide Dog comforted and protected me by assuring me that everything would be all right. I like to feel protected and I especially need that now, and I feel the dog I choose – a St. Bernard – helped to give me that protection. I feel like I'm going into unknown territory, not really sure what I'll do next. But I had that assurance that I was supported whatever happens. So I feel a little more comfortable facing uncertainty."

In Ellen's case, she didn't have a problem now, so she just spent time enjoying being with her Guide Dog and getting to know him better, so she could call on him in the future when needed. As Ellen described it:

"I felt like it was a fun day, and we were there to have fun, play around, and enjoy the weather, because it was nice. So I had a good time throwing balls around, and then my Guide Dog, a big floppy English Sheepdog named Harry, brought them back to me. After that we just lazed around in the sun, and that felt very good. So I didn't have any problem to deal with, but I feel like Harry will be there later when I need some help."

Finally, Paul pointed out that he got some tips from his Guide Dog on how to deal with feelings of stress or anxiety in the future – by doing something to unwind and take his mind off his tension, so it would gradually disappear. As he explained:

"I experienced being stressed out, and when my Guide Dog saw me doing that, he took a tennis ball, came over to me, and shoved it in my hand. Though I wasn't feeling up to it, I got the sense that my Guide Dog, an Irish Setter, was telling me: "I know this is going to be good for you. So throw the tennis ball." Then I did, and I experienced the feelings of stress flowing out of me, and I felt much calmer. So that led me to think that in the future, that's what I need to do: find some activity to release my feelings of tension, even if it's not something I feel like doing at first. But if I do it, that's what's good for me to do. And maybe my Guide Dog will be there to advise me to do it."

Gaining Insights about Another Person

Now the workshop turned to getting insights about another person. While participants could ask their Guide Dog to help, such as by making suggestions on what to think, the goal of the next exercise was to think of some of the people they each knew and think of what dog came to mind and why. "You want to think about, "How well that dog fits each person and what that tells you about them. So now think of somebody in your life, what sort of dog you associate with them, and why."

After everyone shared their reactions, I asked them to reflect on how this information could help them to better deal with that person. As an example, here's my exchange with Andrea, who described her sister as being like a nervous Chihuahua:

Andrea: "I have a sister I associate with a Chihuahua, because she's really nervous and antsy. It's never peaceful being around her. She's always worrying and dealing with some crisis or another. So I guess I picked a Chihuahua to describe her, because they're so scared of something all the time, and they have to continually be reassured that you're their friend and you're not going to hurt them. I think my sister is like that, because she is so nervous, and then she's always trying to suck you into her world, like a Chihuahua."

GSS: "Is there anything about the way you deal with a Chihuahua that would help you deal with your sister?"

Andrea: "Yeah, since Chihuahuas always get so frightened of things, they need to be reassured. You have to make them feel safe and comfortable, such as talking quietly to them a lot, encouraging them to do something, not making quick sudden movements, and not acting like you're going to hurt them, because they're so fragile. My sister's the same way. As I found, you've got to talk to her a lot and not to do anything very quickly before she is agreeable to go along with you on something. She wants to know everything and is really inquisitive, so you have to tell her things and reassure her that everything's going to be okay. And that works with her. Talking to her and reassuring her helps to calm her down."

In David's case, he associated a Dachshund with his ex-wife, feeling the Dachshund's scrappy, snappish behavior fit his wife's personality to a T. Plus, he found the techniques he used to control a Dachshund –isolating it and calming it down, were methods he had used with his ex-wife in the past and would again. Here's how he explained the process:

David: "I thought immediately about my ex-wife and her Dachshund. My wife and I would walk down the street with my other dog and the Dachshund between us, and the Dachshund would walk along with great confidence, always barking and ready to snap at everyone. It was like it was saying: 'Don't mess with me, or I'll sic these other people and their big dog on you.' And my ex-wife is so much like that. She raised that dog from a puppy, and that helped to make the traits common to a Dachshund – being fairly aggressive and snappish – even more common. So it became like a Dachshund with all the unmitigated bad traits of this kind of dog. It's like this Dachshund became scared of everyone. So it barks a lot and bites first, and then tries to make friends. And my ex-wife was very much like that, too."

GGS: "What would be an example of when your ex-wife aced like this?"

David: "Walking through bad neighborhoods, she was like that. She would snap at everyone. For instance, when a bunch of teenagers walked by, she would glare at them with that steely gaze that said: 'Just shut up and walk, don't start anything. Nothing's happening now, so don't let anything happen, or else.'"

So how did David deal with his ex-wife when she became snappish toward him?

David thought one approach was especially applicable, in this and in future relationships:

"With the Dachshund, I took it for a lot of walks, and the way I dealt with its aggressive, snappish behavior, like dealing with my ex-wife, was to create a very controlled environment. For instance, I would take the dog on a fire trail in the park, knowing I'm not liable to run into anyone. So she wouldn't be able to bite and bark at anyone, and in this more controlled setting, she would be more likely to listen to me."

David sometimes used a controlled environment with his ex-wife, as he explained:

David: "With my ex-wife, a controlled environment was not going out. I'd say I'm not going to take you out if you're not going to be nice. Or I would tell her I was too tired. It's too much to do now. Let's rent a movie."

In turn, such suggestions seemed to placate his ex-wife, making her more comfortable and protected in this more isolated setting. David noted:

"I think she sometimes felt like crawling into her shell in fear, but she was more aggressive and extroverted about it. It's like she was putting up her protective barriers by being aggressive in turn to say: 'I feel like something bad is going to happen, but 'm not going let it happen. So don't bother me.'"

Given this insight, David indicated that he planned to be careful about his relationships in the future and avoid getting involved with overly aggressive women.

Sharon, too, felt she had gained some insights about how to be more cautious with people who were very controlling, people who reminded her of some bigger more powerful dogs, like the Mastiff. As she explained:

"I thought of several people I know who are really controlling. They want to control your emotions, personality, and everything about you. They remind me of a very big dominant type of dog, who is really scary to be around. In the future, I need to be more cautious about being sucked in by such people. So if someone makes me think of such a big tough dog in the future, like a Mastiff or Presa Canario, that's a sign I need to be more careful and not get caught up in such a relationship.

Getting First Impressions

Then, the focus of the workshop shifted to first impressions. The question was: What associations with different dogs come to mind when you first meet someone and how might that help you relate to that person? Here are some highlights of these discussions.

Andrea, a dog owner, used these associations to help her decide whether to get to know a person better. As she described it:

"When I met a friendly person, an outgoing person, I think of a dog that is like very outgoing and happy, like a Pomeranian, Labrador, or Irish Setter. They seem happy and can fit in with anything. When you meet people like that, you get a good rapport with them, like they're someone you want to be around. Or when you meet people that are lovable and you just want to hug them, the dog that comes to mind is a St. Bernard. They're so warm and lovable."

David described how he was particularly drawn to people who reminded him of mixed breeds, and commonly these people owned mixed breeds, too.

"When I meet anyone, I correlate them with dogs. So I'm drawn to someone I think of as a mixed breed person, which means to me someone who is different, unique. They can't be put in a box, so I think of them as more adaptable and creative. And some can be very warm and friendly. For example, I was thinking of my friend's mixed breed dog, Rug. He lays on the floor a lot, and the kids love to play with him. It's like they're all part of the pack, so there's no real barrier between the dog and the kids. When I think of people as mixed breeds, that's the feeling I get – that they'll fit in and want to connect with many different types of people. They're not just tied to one breed."

Apart from getting their own impressions on meeting people, the participants thought asking the question: "What kind of dog do you like or like most?" would be a great opener. It would be a way to better understand the person right away, and it could get them to open up more about themselves.

In fact, Andrea had already asked this question when she met people in learning if they were dog owners. As she explained: "Sometimes people have approached me on the street when I'm walking my dog to ask about her. Then, it'll come up in conversation, when I ask them: Do you have a dog? I'll also ask them, 'What kind of dog do you like, and then they'll tell me.'"

Then by asking them questions, she found people more open. "When you ask a person that question that seems to open them up. They start thinking about the qualities they like in a dog and why, so you have some insights about what they would be like. You don't even have to ask them why they like that dog. They'll explain it themselves, and you can see their emotions by the expressions in their face. You can also tell if they're a dog owner. Or if they don't have a dog, you can tell what kind they would like to get if they do."

In Ellen's view, asking a question would help her in forming first impressions. As Ellen described:

> "I think an answer would help you gain an immediate insight about who that person is and how to relate to them. Later, you can always check out those impressions once you get to know someone. And usually they will be correct, because when people tell you what dog they like the most, that will express how they feel, and what they are really like, without them thinking about the question or trying to impress you. They'll come right out and let you know, because it's easy to state a preference for a kind of dog. Then, as you get to know them, you can see them act out those feelings. So just by the little a person tells you about what dog they like, you'll have a more real picture of who they are, and so you can be more trusting of them."

Apart from gaining insights into others, the participants also thought asking the question could be a great conversation starter and then a good way for people to get to know each other.

An Exercise on Getting First Impressions

Our next exercise focused on getting first impressions throughout the day. While it can be good practice to do this in reality – say you come up with quick reactions as you pass people on the street, this technique involved visualizing a series of encounters from morning to night and coming up with an association for each person they met. As I explained the process:

"In this next exercise, you'll go through your day to day activities, where you'll visualize the people you meet and notice what kind of dog comes to mind. This exercise is something which you could do in reality whatever you do that day.

For example, say you go into a supermarket. When you check out with the supermarket clerk, notice what image of a dog comes to mind.

We'll do this as a visualization in which I'll lead you to different places where you will participate in various activities throughout the day Along the way, you'll visualize the people you meet and the different dogs you associate with them."

After everyone was ready to do the exercise, I began as follows:

Just get very calm and relaxed. Now imagine you are in your house getting up, ready to start your day.

Now you're dressed, ready to go out, and you're going to take a walk around the neighborhood. So go outside, and as you walk, notice who you meet. As you meet or pass by each person, just imagine what kind of dog they are. See the image of the dog come to mind and notice the personality of the dog and the person. And think what about the person suggests that type of dog.

So take that walk now, and I'll be quiet for about a minute while you do...

Now I'd like you to imagine that it's lunchtime, and you're going into a local restaurant. As you do, the waitress or waiter comes over or you see the person behind the counter, and you get an impression of them as a dog. What kind of dog would that be?

Now you have a friend who's meeting you there. You see your friend come in, and he or she sits down with you. As you greet your friend and talk, imagine what kind of dog that friend would be. Then, notice the qualities you associate with that dog and that person...

Now you're finishing lunch, and you're going to take the afternoon off to do a fun thing you like to do — like going to the park, to the zoo, or for a boat ride. As you do whatever you want, you meet people along the way. And you associate different kinds of dogs with these people. See what comes to mind, and how the characteristics of the dog or person you meet fit with that person...

Now you're returning from what you were doing in the afternoon, and you're going to go to an after-hours cocktail party. It could be at a friend's house, at a business club, at a local night club. You go in and meet some people there. These may be the bartender, some people you socialize with. Again notice who these people are and what kinds of dogs you associate with them. Then, notice the personality characteristics that come to mind...

Now before you go home, you're going to relax in a movie theater. As you watch any movie you'd like to see, and see the actors and actresses on the screen, you see the image of a dog associated with actors or actresses. Again, just notice what personality characteristics they have which you associate with the dog...

Now you see yourself leaving the movie theater going home. You're feeling very relaxed, very good, having had a very nice, interesting day. You go into your house and sink into an easy chair or couch. And you're feeling really good, as you return to everyday reality.

A Day of Seeing Dogs

Once everyone was back from the visualization, I asked people to share their experiences. Here are the highlights of their comments.

David: "The experience made me more aware about the breeds of dogs, and especially their body language, since one breed can look like the other, but their personalities are very different. That's what happened when I went through my day.

"I was doing field interview work for the marketing company I worked for, and I met a range of people with different personality types – much like I do at work. For instance, when I came up to some of the houses, some of the people had a watch dog, and it was going: "raahh, raaah, raaah."But after the owner introduced the watch dog to me, all of sudden, I was part of the family, and the dog stopped barking at me and tried to be friendly."

GSS: "Did you see any associations of the dogs and personality types as you met different people through the day?

David: "Yeah, I noticed that the mannerisms and temperaments of the different people I met went along with certain types of dogs. For instance, the tough guy in the underwear who answered the door had a Boston Terrier, and a teenage girl in a short mini shirt had a small yapping Yorkie. So definitely, yes, there was a strong connection though I also noticed, with dogs, as with people, after they feel okay with you, say you're doing research, not trying to sell them anything, they get more relaxed and friendly. So I experienced a lot of personality change, as I went from house to house.

Then, David reported briefly on his other experiences.

"In the lunch room, I saw a woman sitting at a booth in the back, who was like a Great Dane, sitting there in a confident and friendly way.

"And at a cocktail party, the people reminded me of dogs sniffing at each other, or they milled around sniffing at each other, trying to decide who to go home with for the night. You've got basically 30 seconds to convince someone you're a great person, so the other person will want to keep you around, or they're on to meet someone else. This quaint interchange is a lot like what dogs do. If they don't like the smell of another dog, that's too bad. They take off and they're gone.

"And then I met a waitress at a nightclub, who was a real Bassett-Hound type, which means that she was a really good waitress, loyal and devoted just like a friendly Bassett.

"Then at the movies I visualized Clint Eastwood as a Coon Hound, and Robert Redford, like a Springer Spaniel or English Setter. Why? I think I saw Eastwood like this dog because he seems like a hunter, a guy that's strong, confident, always on the prowl, and he's good at sniffing out dishonesty and anger. And Redford? Well, he's got that friendly, outdoorsy, family quality about him, and I think of these dogs as being like that."

Here's what Andrea had to say about the matches she found with women in the street, a writer, and a friend bartender.

"I started out going to the bank, and I met this woman who was walking down the street. I saw her earlier today and tonight I visualized her even more clearly. She really stood out, because this is a blue collar neighborhood, but she was dressed elegantly and was very confident. Then, I noticed that she had this dog, like a Yorkie Terrier, which she carried under her arm like a purse, and this dog looked very confident like her. It seemed to be proud to be there, like it knew it was on display and really fit there. It looked like she picked that dog, because it looked good with her, like an accessory.

"So as she walked along, she seemed very proud and arrogant and didn't look at anybody, and just like I sensed earlier, she didn't want to talk to anyone, which was like a confirmation that I was right to not say anything to compliment her earlier that day. It's like both in reality and in my visualization, when I looked at her, she looked away, like she didn't want me or anyone else to intrude on her space. And her dog looked away, too, just like her. So it was a perfect match.

"Then at the restaurant, when a waiter wearing a tie came over to me, a boxer came to mind, because boxers are such slick, neat dogs, and I've seen pictures of boxers wearing ties. Then when my friend sat down at the table, I pictured a Labrador…I guess because Labradors are a very relaxed and friendly, and that's what my friend is like.

"Later, at the park, I saw dogs and people running around, everyone having a good time. And the dogs I envisioned there were like Setters and mixed breed dogs, because when I think of those dogs, I think of everyone enjoying the outdoors and having fun.

"Next, at the club I saw a bartender who reminded me of a Doberman, because they're both tough. Or maybe, I thought, he might be more like a Rottweiler, because he seemed really controlled as he looked around, checking what everyone else was doing, to see that customers were being treated properly and everything was going smoothly.

"Then, as I looked around the club, I thought of Poodles and Collies for the women there, because they were dressed up and showing off. After that, in the movie, as I watched a comedy, I thought of mixed breeds for some of the comedians. I imagined a shaggy dog, because the comedians were dressed like that. Finally, when I was relaxing at home, I imagined a Shepherd or Collie was there with me, because I live in a tough neighborhood, and a Shepherd or Collie could be my protector. "

And so, as each person went through their day, they experienced multiple images of dogs associated with many different types of people, and it almost always was a good match.

So now, as I explained, they could apply this technique in everyday life. "Here's how you can apply the method every day.

As you go around during the day, notice what associations you have with the different people in your life. Or when you see people on the street, think of the first dog that comes to mind. Later, if you can, check out your perceptions with the people for whom you make these associations. You'll find the more you work with these associations, the more sensitive you will get. And when you share this information, it's a great conversational opener and a great way to know the people you already know even better."

Learning from the Dog Associations

Then, the conversation turned to how people might learn from their associations to guide their interactions with others, such as knowing when to avoid certain people or situations, as Ellen and Paul reported:

Ellen: "I was just being carefree (during the visualization) and I saw a retriever. It was a nice friendly dog that I liked to be around and felt perfectly safe with. Then, I thought about how if a dog seemed like it was going to be vicious, I would steer away from it. How would I know? By looking at its body language, such as raising its hackles to show it was getting ready for attack.

"Then, that got me thinking about what to look for in people to know if I wanted to be with them or not. For example, I saw some people I knew I would stay away from because their expression showed they didn't want to be bothered. So I bypassed them to keep them from interfering with my happy mood.

Paul: "I thought about getting cues on who or what to avoid, too. The visualization was like a reminder to pay more attention to this and be careful. For instance, I saw people when walking around with my dog, where I could tell by reading their body language that I didn't want to be around them, because they might be dangerous. Then, my dog signaled me by tugging on its leash, saying: "Let's go this way." Likewise, when my own dog sees a dog he knows is a problem, he'll avoid it. He'll shy away indicating that 'I'm scared of that dog. Let's go this way.'"

As Paul and Ellen's experience suggested, it's important to pay attention to the dog images and associations to better get to know others and decide what to do as a result. As I explained:

"Say you are walking down the street, see some people ahead of you and get an image of your dog tugging on its leash. That's a message from your unconscious to avoid the situation, perhaps by walking on the other side of the block or finding another route. You get such messages from your unconscious in the form of sudden feelings of tension or anxiety. Then, the images and associates you get by working with these techniques magnify those messages, so they are clearer and you pay more attention to them."

What about the problem of getting mixed messages? How do you interpret the signals then, David wondered. As he noted: "Sometimes the body language of dogs is contradictory. Usually, you can tell when a dog's hackles are up that he's ready to attack. But sometimes dogs have their hackles up, but their tail wagging, so they appear friendly. Then, you get close, and boom, they really love to attack. So they're just drawing you in and putting you off your guard."

David's image of real-life experiences during the visualization suggested the need for extra caution, not only with dogs showing these contradictory signs with these same characteristics.

"I've had an experience in offices with backstabbers, and I can imagine a number of dogs that might be like that, such as a Pit Bull who's friendly as long as you keep him fed and happy. But once you slip up on a meal, watch out. You could

be the next victim. Backstabbers are like that, too.
They just wait for the right opportunity. Then,
boom, they plunge in the knife."

"That's right," I said, wrapping up the discussion with a last comment. "By being sensitive to these different kinds of dogs, you become sensitive to the type of people who might be like that – people who are tail wagging, yet ready to attack you. So if you sense these mixed signals, such as while you're talking to this person and the image of a tail-wagging dog ready to pounce comes to mind, you know it's time to put up your defenses. Or maybe you might even try a pre-emptive offensive, since you're dealing with someone you can't trust."

Making Changes in a Relationship

The workshop concluded with two exercises on changing a situation. One was to create a warmer, personal relationship or reduce tension in a conflict by sending warm feelings to another person. The other was to increase one's feelings of power and confidence in a relationship.

As I explained the process:

"In this first visualization, you will imagine you are sending feelings of love, affection, or warmth to a person you want to feel closer to or overcome a conflict with using the help of your Power Dog or Guide Dog. Then, in the visualization on increasing your power in a relationship, you will imagine your Power Dog coming with you to help."

After each visualization, there was a brief discussion about what each person experienced and how to apply that experience in everyday life.

For example, after the "Sending Love" visualization, Sharon described turning to a St. Bernard for help, because, "They're so big and lovable." Though Sharon didn't have any particular person in mind, she felt she could use the technique to meet someone in a more receptive frame of mind. As she commented:

"This might be a good approach to create a warmer, more comfortable setting for a date or romantic encounter. But I want to do this in a restrained, controlled way, since you could overwhelm someone if you send out your feelings too intensely. You don't want to come on too strong."

Finally, I set the stage for the last visualization about increasing one's power in a relationship.

"Now, to increase your power, you'll see yourself as being very powerful. You'll also call on your Power Dog, a dog you associate with being powerful, to make you feel even more powerful. Then, you'll see yourself in the relationship or situation where you want this additional power. You'll imagine a scene that is likely to happen, you'll express this newly found sense of power there. Later, when you are with that person or in that situation for real, you'll carry those increased feelings of power with you, and you'll be better able to act to express that power."

After the visualization, there was a final discussion about everyone's experience and how to apply this feeling of greater power in their situations. This time everyone chose work situations, since that was the setting in which one is most concerned with power in relationships. "It's where alpha and beta are most relevant – at work, Paul observed, "Either you're on top or somebody else is, and you want to know."

How did everyone feel they could apply their experience of power in the workplace? Here are some highlights from the discussion.

Paul: "After the experience of being more powerful, I imagined being at work dealing with my boss. At first, I saw my boss as being very snappy as before, and then I saw myself saying things to her before she could say them to me, because I knew she would say them. I wanted to say them first, because if she did, she would take control, and if she did, that would be unsettling. But if I could say them first, I could take control. So it was a little like my boss and I were playing a power game, like "Who goes first?" But this was my way of pulling out the rug from under her by saying what she expected to say first. For instance, I'd tell her: 'Okay, I know how well I did, which wasn't enough, and I know I have to do better.'

"Afterwards, I worked on adding power to my response, so in the future I would feel even stronger and better able to stand up to her."

Then, Paul had even more ideas about ways of working with his boss in the future.

Paul: "Besides standing up to her, I could find a more creative way of working with her and take on more responsibility. For example, one image that came to mind is of my sled dog pulling the sled up to the problem, identifying it, and thinking of the quickest and easiest way around it. So increasing power doesn't always mean having a confrontation with someone. It's more about working smarter and independently and being able to do more myself. So I think that would be a better strategy to use – the way of the sled dog, rather than playing the pit bull and getting knocked out of the ring."

As I commented: "One way this process can work is when you haven't expressed this power before in a relationship. Visualizing this gives you a charge of power so you feel ready to go do it. It's also a way to identify different possibilities in advance so you can try them out mentally. The process helps you feel like you can do almost anything, since you're safe to imagine it now. Then, in reality, you can do it or not. But since you have gone through that scenario before, you are prepared if that's a good way to act. It's like a pre-exercise. Plus the process adds an extra charge of power, since you are associating your Power Dog with it."

Andrea had exactly that experience, explaining that: "My Power Dog was a Doberman. They know how to sit quietly in the corner, just watching and feeling out what different people are like, like they are preparing their strategy on how to respond and how much power to use if they are called on to attack. So they are not too overpowering or use too little power. So they have a power they can control, and I would like that kind of power myself. That's why I chose a Doberman as my Power Dog. It's a dog that can be controlled, but has a lot of power and is watchful."

GSS: "And then you take that image and experience with you to remind yourself how to exercise your own power and control, and that reinforces how you want to act."

By contrast, David chose a Power Dog he associated with using more subterfuge to exercise power. As he described his experience, "My Power Dog was a sled dog, and I thought about how the Alpha Beta dynamic is very strong in work relationships, like in a dog pack, where the top dog wants all the other dogs to know who's the most powerful. So if you're not the Alpha dog but you want to get what you want, you have to do this in a more roundabout way. I do field work doing interviews in the neighborhoods, so I don't have to be around the boss. So I imagined this sled dog in the snow getting the ball to the goal while avoiding the boss. The other dogs were still hooked up to the sled, so they were going along with pack leader, but my dog was out on his own, so he had the power to be free.

I explained, "A sled dog is the perfect example of this more surreptitious use of power and that many sled dogs may be part of the pack and learn to follow the lead dog, but they can be very independent and stubborn, like Siberian Huskies. So if they don't respect the dog or person exercising authority or you open the door, out they go. And it sounds like your boss is very much like this."

David: "Yes, she is. She may still own the sled, but I can find ways to get where I am without being hooked up to it. That approach works well for me, so that's what I'll keep doing."

On that note, the workshop ended, with everyone eager to apply their experiences with their Guide Dogs and Power Dogs in their real life work situation, though Paul had one last question as he flipped through the profiles of different types of dogs.

"What if you don't see an association you have with a particular dog listed as a personality trait, and you're trying to imagine a better way to relate to that person?"

"That doesn't matter," I explained. "The associations listed are the ones most commonly thought to characterize that dog. But what's important is not the images that others have, but your own associations with each dogs. Think of the ones that are listed as a way to get you started thinking about the common characteristics of these different dogs. Then, add your own trait – whether for your Power Dog or the person you are working or interacting with. Then, use these associations – the common ones and your own – to help you both increase your feelings of power and decide the best approach to use in drawing on your power in that situation to better get what you want in that relationship."

Setting Up Your Own Workshop

Here are some tips for setting up your own workshop.
- Start off with an introduction on using the Guide Dogs for getting advice.
- After participants choose their Guide Dogs, ask everyone to describe the dog they chose, why, and how their Guide Dog helped them.
- Ask people to think about the people in their life and the dogs they associate with them.
- Discuss how people can apply these associations to make changes in relationships.
- Invite people to share about their experiences or their reactions to others' experiences or ask questions.
- Have fun.

ABOUT THE AUTHOR

GINI GRAHAM SCOTT, Ph.D., J.D., is a nationally known writer, consultant, speaker, and seminar leader, specializing in social trends, popular culture, business and work relationships, and professional and personal development. She has published over 50 books on diverse subjects with major publishers. She has worked with dozens of clients on memoirs, self-help, and popular business books, as well as film scripts. Her websites include www.changemakerspublishingandwriting.com and www.ginigrahamscott.com. She is a Huffington Post regular columnist, commenting on social trends, new technology, business, and everyday life at www.huffingtonpost.com/gini-graham-scott.

She is the founder of Changemakers Publishing featuring books on social trends, work, business, psychology, and self-help, which has published over 100 Print, e-books, and audiobooks. She has licensed several dozen books for foreign sales, including in the UK, Russia, Korea, Spain, Indonesia, and Japan.

She has written numerous books on creativity and visualization, including *Mind Power: Picture Your Way to Success; The Empowered Mind: How to Harness the Creative Force within You;* and *Want It, See It, Get It!*

She has received national media exposure for her books, including appearances on *Good Morning America, Oprah,* and *CNN.* She has been the producer and host of a talk show series, CHANGEMAKERS, featuring interviews on social trends.

Scott is active in a number of community and business groups, including the Lafayette, Danville, and Pleasant Hill Chambers of Commerce. She is a graduate of the prestigious Leadership in Contra Costa County program and is a member of a BNI group in Walnut Creek, B2B groups in Danville and Walnut Creek, and many other business networking groups. She is the organizer of six Meetup groups in the film and publishing industries with over 6000 members in Los Angeles and the San Francisco Bay Area. She also does workshops and seminars on the topics of her books.

She received her Ph.D. from the University of California, Berkeley, and her J.D. from the University of San Francisco Law School. She has received five MAs at Cal State, East Bay, including most recently an MA in Communications. She will be starting an additional MA program in history there in the fall of 2017.

CHANGEMAKERS PUBLISHING
3527 Mt. Diablo Blvd., #273
Lafayette, CA 94549
changemakers@pacbell.net . (925) 385-0608
www.changemakerspublishingandwriting.com

www.ingramcontent.com/pod-product-compliance
Lightning Source LLC
Chambersburg PA
CBHW071538080526
44588CB00011B/1712